The Big Book of
BIBLE
QUESTIONS

Sally Ann Wright and Paola Bertolini Grudina

CONTENTS

3.75

CREATION

Q Who made the world?

A God did!

In the beginning, there was nothing.

God made the sea and sky and filled the land with fruit-bearing trees and flowering plants. God filled the sea with silvery fish and the sky with birds that soared through the air.

God made all the different creatures and people just like us, who could think and feel and love.

God saw that all God made was very good.

Q What did the people do wrong?

A They disobeyed God.

God gave a beautiful world to the people God had made. God asked them to name all the animals and look after the world. There was only one thing God told them not to do. They could eat anything they liked, except for the fruit from one tree.

But the serpent tempted Eve, and Eve tempted Adam, and when they had disobeyed God, they all blamed each other.

Q Why did Adam and Eve hide from God?

A They were ashamed.

Adam and Eve realized that they had done something wrong.

First, they clothed themselves with fig leaves from the trees around them. Then they hid from God. Adam and Eve felt guilty and knew they had spoiled all the good things God had given them.

God was sad that Adam and Eve could not be trusted anymore. The perfect world was perfect no longer.

Q When did the angels come?

A When Adam and Eve were banished from the garden of Eden.

God clothed the people with animal skins and told them that they must leave the garden and go and cultivate the land somewhere else. They would no longer be able to live forever, but would live, work, have children, and die.

Then God put angels outside the garden and a flaming sword that moved back and forth to prevent them from returning. Adam and Eve knew that they could no longer be called God's friends.

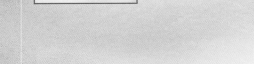

NOAH

Q Why did God send a flood?

A To wash away all the evil in the world.

When God made the world, everything was good. But as more and more people lived on the earth, they started to forget that God had made them.

They lied and stole from each other. They fought and killed each other. They did terrible things so that God wished God had never made them at all.

Q What did Noah build?

A An ark!

Noah was the only man who remembered God and listened to God.

God told Noah to build a big boat, an ark, that would float on the floodwaters. God gave Noah careful measurements. God told him to make the ark out of cypress wood and cover it with pitch to make it waterproof.

Then Noah had to take his wife, his family, and two of every kind of creature onto the ark, so they would not be destroyed by the floodwaters.

Q For how long
did it rain?

A For forty days and forty
nights.

God had told Noah to take enough food to feed all the creatures that were packed onto the ark. Noah and his wife, his three sons—Shem, Ham, and Japheth—and their three wives cared for the animals while it rained. The floodwaters rose and destroyed everything outside.

When the rain stopped, it took months for the water to go down and the earth to dry up.

Q Where
did the ark come to rest?

A On Mount Ararat.

Noah sent out a raven and then a dove to see if they should come out of the ark. After the dove had returned with an olive leaf in its beak, God told Noah it was safe to let all the animals out of the ark.

Noah thanked God for keeping them safe. God sent a beautiful rainbow as a reminder of God's promise never again to destroy the earth by flood.

ABRAHAM

Q Why did Abraham leave his home?

A God told him to!

God promised to make Abraham the father of a great nation with many descendants. But first Abraham had to leave his home.

Abraham trusted God. He took his wife and servants, sheep and goats, and all his belongings and went where God took him.

Q Where did God take Abraham?

A To Canaan, the Promised Land.

Abraham went from his home in a place called Ur to Canaan, a rich and fertile land.

When he got there, his nephew, Lot, went to live on the plains of the River Jordan. Abraham stayed with his own flocks of sheep and goats in Canaan, and made his home there.

Abraham and his family lived in tents. They had everything they needed in the land God gave them.

Q What did God promise Abraham?

A A baby son.

Abraham and Sarah were growing older and they still had no son of their own. But God promised that it would happen.

One day three visitors, sent by God, came to Abraham's tents.

When the visitors left, they promised Abraham that Sarah would soon be holding her child. It happened just as they said. Baby Isaac was born the next year.

Q Who was Isaac's wife?

A Rebekah.

Abraham sent his servant on a journey to find a wife for Isaac from among Abraham's people.

The servant prayed that God would show him the right woman. He prayed that she would come and offer him water from the well. She would then water all ten of his thirsty camels.

Rebekah did exactly that. She went back with the servant to become Isaac's wife.

JACOB

Q Who had twin sons?

A Isaac and Rebekah.

Esau was the firstborn, a hairy child who grew up to be a good hunter. Jacob was second and was born holding Esau's heel. Esau was Isaac's favorite son, but Rebekah liked Jacob best.

One day Esau came home from hunting and demanded some of the lentil stew that Jacob was cooking. Jacob agreed to give him some, as long as Esau gave up his right to the blessing that was always given to the firstborn son.

Q Why did Jacob cover himself with animal skins?

A So Isaac would think he was Esau!

When Isaac was old and almost blind, he told Esau he wanted to bless him.

Esau went hunting so he could prepare his father his favorite meal.

Instead, Rebekah helped Jacob to cook the meal. Then she covered Jacob's arms and neck with animal skins so he would feel and smell like his older brother.

Isaac blessed Jacob instead of Esau. When Esau found out, Jacob had to run away and hide for fear that his brother would kill him!

Q What did Jacob dream?

A Of a stairway leading to heaven.

Jacob ran to his Uncle Laban. On the way he found a place to sleep. There he dreamed...

In his dream he saw a stairway leading from earth to heaven. Angels went up and down the stairway, and God was at the top. God promised to look after Jacob wherever he went and one day to lead him back to Canaan. God promised to bless Jacob's family so they would become the great nation that God had promised to Abraham, Jacob's grandfather.

Q How did Laban cheat Jacob?

A By making him marry Leah.

Jacob fell in love with Rachel, Laban's younger daughter. Laban promised that Jacob could marry Rachel if he worked for him for seven years.

At the end of seven years, Laban tricked Jacob into marrying Leah, his older daughter. After they were married, Laban agreed that Jacob could marry Rachel as well, as long as he worked another seven years afterwards.

JOSEPH

Q What did Joseph wear?

A A beautiful colored coat.

Joseph was the first son of his mother, Rachel, whom Jacob loved very much. But Jacob also had eleven other sons and a daughter. When he treated Joseph as his favorite son and gave him a special coat, he made the other children very jealous.

Q Who sold Joseph into slavery?

A Joseph's older brothers.

First they plotted to kill Joseph. They threw him into an empty well while they decided what to do.

Then some Midianite traders passed by, carrying spices and other goods to be sold in Egypt. The brothers sold Joseph to the traders for twenty pieces of silver. The traders tied Joseph up and took him away to sell as a slave.

Q When was Joseph in prison?

A After Potiphar's wife told lies.

Joseph worked in Potiphar's house in Egypt until Potiphar's wife told lies about him and Joseph was thrown into prison.

Joseph worked hard for the master of the prison. Soon he was looking after the other prisoners.

God had plans for Joseph. After a while, Pharaoh's baker and cupbearer were also imprisoned.

Q Why was Joseph set free?

A He could understand dreams!

God showed Joseph the meaning of the dreams that troubled Pharaoh's baker and cupbearer. One was set free and the other was executed, just as Joseph had told them.

When Pharaoh had bad dreams, Joseph was brought out of prison to help him. Joseph warned that there would be seven years of good harvests followed by seven years of famine. Pharaoh put Joseph in charge of storing all the grain.

MOSES IN EGYPT

Q Who rescued the baby in the basket?

A Pharaoh's daughter, an Egyptian princess.

Moses had been hidden in a basket in the River Nile because Pharaoh wanted all Hebrew baby boys killed. Pharaoh thought there were too many Israelites in Egypt. They were useful as slaves, but he was afraid they would rebel against him.

Baby Moses was found by Pharaoh's daughter. She let him live in the palace and treated him as her son.

Q What was on fire in the desert?

A A burning bush!

Moses had left the palace and was living in the desert of Midian. He was looking after his father-in-law's sheep when he saw the bush that seemed to be on fire – but was not burning up. When he went closer, Moses saw an angel. Then God told Moses to go to Pharaoh and tell him that he must free the Israelite slaves.

Q When did God send the plagues?

A When Pharaoh refused to let the people go.

Moses went to Pharaoh, but he would not let God's people go.

Moses touched the River Nile with his staff, and the water turned to blood. But still Pharaoh would not let his slaves go. There were plagues of frogs, gnats, flies, a plague on livestock, boils on the people, hail, locusts, and darkness over all the land. Pharaoh begged Moses to take the plagues away, but when God did, Pharaoh changed his mind.

Q Why did Pharaoh give in?

A All the firstborn in the land died.

The tenth plague was the death of the first child or animal in every family. The Israelites had been told by God to pack everything and to be ready to leave. They ate one last meal, the Passover meal. They put the blood of the lamb they ate on their doorposts so the angel of death would pass over their houses.

Pharaoh's own son died with all the others. Then Pharaoh told Moses to take his people, their sheep and cattle and silver and gold, and leave Egypt.

MOSES IN THE DESERT

Q How did Moses cross the Red Sea?

A God parted the waters.

In the form of a pillar of cloud by day and a pillar of fire by night, God led the people. When they reached the sea, the people were afraid, but God told Moses to stretch out his staff over the sea. The waters parted so that the Israelites could cross over to the other side.

Q Who tried to follow the Israelites?

A The Egyptians.

As soon as Pharaoh had let the Israelites go, he changed his mind again. He prepared his chariots and soldiers to bring them back.

When the Israelites had crossed safely to the other side of the sea, Moses held out his staff, and the waters returned. They flowed over Pharaoh's armies so that the Israelites were free.

Q **Where were ten laws given?**

A **On Mount Sinai.**

God wrote the laws, the Ten Commandments, on two stone tablets and gave them to Moses. These laws

showed God's people how to live. They were to worship and love the one true God. They were also to respect other people so that they could live together as God intended—not stealing or murdering or wanting anything that belonged to another.

As long as they followed these commandments, God promised to lead God's people and care for them and take them to a land of their own.

Q **What did the people eat in the desert?**

A **Quail and manna.**

It was not long before the Israelites started to complain that they were hungry and thirsty and wished they were slaves again!

God caused clean water to flow from a rock and provided quail to fly over them so they could catch them and have meat. Every day God provided "manna," which tasted like honey. God gave them all they needed, day by day.

THE PROMISED LAND

Q What was the name of the Promised Land?

A Canaan.

God had promised Abraham that his descendants would one day live in Canaan, where there were plenty of good things to eat.

Moses led God's people out of Egypt, but he died before the people settled in the Promised Land.

Q Who led the Israelites after Moses' death?

A Joshua.

Joshua had already been in the Promised Land as one of the spies sent out by Moses. Only Joshua and Caleb believed that God would help them to make their home there. All the other spies were afraid of the people who lived in Canaan.

Q Where did Rahab live?

A In Jericho.

Joshua sent spies into Jericho before attacking the city. Rahab hid the spies under the flax on her rooftop so the king's men would not find them. Later she let them out through the window, as her house was built into the city wall.

Rahab knew that God would help the Israelites take the city and asked them to promise to save her and her family. She put a red cord in the window so they knew where she was.

Q How many priests marched with trumpets?

A Seven priests.

God told Joshua that the walls of Jericho would fall down if they followed God's instructions. Seven priests blew on trumpets as they marched around the city for six days. An armed guard marched in front of them. An armed guard marched behind them. In between, priests carried the ark of the covenant.

On the seventh day they all marched seven times around. On the seventh march, the people shouted, and the walls of the city fell down. Only Rahab and her family were saved.

JUDGES

Q When did the chariots get stuck in the mud?

A In the time of Deborah.

The cruel Canaanite King, Jabin, made life very difficult for the Israelites. So God told Deborah that she should send Barak with an army to fight against him.

Barak was afraid and wouldn't go alone, so Deborah went with him against Sisera, Jabin's commander. Sisera brought 900 chariots to the battle. But God was on the side of the Israelites. God sent down rain and the river flooded. The chariot wheels got stuck in the mud, and the Israelites won the battle.

Q Where did Gideon hide?

A In the wine press.

Gideon was threshing wheat in the wine press so that the Israelites' enemies, the Midianites, could not see him and steal it from him.

An angel came to Gideon there and told him that God wanted him to lead God's people against the Midianites. Gideon could hardly believe that God had chosen him to save God's people! Gideon was neither brave nor important! But God helped Gideon so that he won a victory with a very small army of men.

Q Who fought a lion
with his bare hands?

A Samson.

Samson was a very strong man. As
long as he kept his vows to God and
did not have his hair cut, he would
remain stronger than any other man.
This was his secret.

One day, he was attacked by a lion.
Samson fought the lion and was able
to save himself and kill the lion without
any weapon but his hands.

Q How did Samson die?

A The walls of the Philistine
temple fell on him.

The Philistines asked Delilah to find
out the secret of Samson's strength.

Delilah tricked Samson into telling
his secret that his hair
must not be cut. Delilah
betrayed him to the
Philistines. When they cut
off Samson's hair, God's
power left him. He was
captured and blinded.

Samson asked God to
give him back his strength one more
time. He pulled down the pillars of the
temple so that thousands of Philistines
died with him that day.

SAMUEL

Q Why did Hannah weep?

A She wanted to have a child of her own.

Hannah's husband, Elkanah, had two wives. Elkanah loved Hannah very much but she had no children. His other wife had sons and daughters.

Hannah prayed for a son of her own. She promised to give her child back to God to serve in the temple. God answered her prayer, and Hannah was overjoyed when she gave birth to Samuel.

Q When did God call to Samuel?

A At night.

As soon as he was old enough, Samuel worked alongside the priest, Eli, in the temple. One night, God called Samuel's name. Samuel thought Eli was calling and went to him. After the third time, Eli realized that God was calling Samuel. He told the boy to answer, "Speak, Lord, for your servant is listening."

Q How many brothers did David have?

A Seven.

Samuel went to the house of a man called Jesse and asked to see all his sons.

All seven were good strong men. But God did not choose any of these to be king after Saul. Samuel asked if Jesse had another son. The youngest son was looking after his father's sheep.

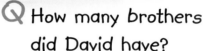

God told Samuel that this son, David, was the man God wanted to be king.

Q Whom did Samuel anoint first King of Israel?

A Saul.

When the people said they wanted to be like the other nations, God told Samuel that God would choose a King for the Israelites. When Saul came to Samuel asking for help to find Saul's lost donkeys, Samuel knew that Saul was the man God had chosen. And Samuel anointed him.

DAVID

Q What instrument did David play?

A The harp.

King Saul was often bad tempered or depressed. David first went to work in the King's service in order to play his harp to soothe Saul.

David composed songs called psalms and played the harp when he sang them. Some psalms praised God's greatness. Others expressed that David was sorry or needed God's help.

Q Who was Goliath?

A The champion for the Philistines.

Goliath was a giant of a man, over nine feet tall. He wore a bronze helmet and bronze body armor. His legs were protected with bronze greaves and he carried a bronze javelin and a spear with a heavy iron point.

Every morning and every evening he taunted the Israelites and told them to send a champion to fight him.

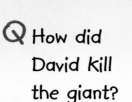

Q Why did King Saul want to lend David his armor?

A So David could fight Goliath.

All the soldiers from King Saul's army were afraid. So David went to King Saul.

David said that God, who had saved him from the paw of the lion and bear when he had been protecting his sheep, would save him from Goliath. David would fight the giant.

King Saul tried to make David wear his armor and take his sword, but it was all too big and heavy. David said he would go without it.

Q How did David kill the giant?

A With a sling and a stone.

David chose five smooth stones from the stream and went out to meet Goliath with his sling in his hand. The Philistine champion told him to approach and die.

"You have a sword and a spear," David told Goliath, "but I have God on my side. Soon you will know that there is a God in Israel!"

David's stone hit Goliath on his forehead and the giant fell down dead. God had given David the victory!

SOLOMON

Q What gift did God give to Solomon?

A Wisdom.

When David's son Solomon became King, he had a dream. He dreamed that God asked him to choose any gift he wanted. Solomon did not choose money or long life or power. He chose wisdom so that he could lead his people well.

God was so pleased with Solomon's answer that God gave Solomon wisdom and riches too.

Q Why did Solomon ask for a baby to be cut in half?

A To find the baby's mother.

Two women came to Solomon with one baby. Each one said the baby was hers.

Solomon ordered a soldier to cut the baby in half so each woman could have half a baby! One mother agreed; the other said she would rather give her baby away than see it die.

Solomon knew then who the real mother was. He gave the baby to the woman who would not let it die.

Q Where did God's people worship?

A In the Temple.

Solomon chose the finest timber and the best craftsmen. He decorated the Temple with beautiful carved figures covered with gold.

Solomon knew that God was too great to live in the Temple, but he asked God to listen when people came there to pray. God promised to hear their prayers, as long as the people agreed to obey God.

Q Who came to visit King Solomon?

A The queen of Sheba.

Everyone heard about Solomon's wisdom and wealth and many came to visit him, but the queen of Sheba came a long way across the desert to test him. She brought many gifts, such as gold and precious stones and expensive spices, with her on camels.

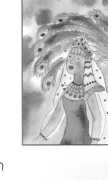

When she had been with Solomon some time, the queen of Sheba agreed that God had blessed him and that no one could be wiser than Solomon.

ELIJAH

Q Why did God send a drought?

A To punish King Ahab.

Ahab had been worshiping the idols of his wife, Jezebel, including Baal, who was supposed to be the god of rain.

God told Elijah to warn Ahab that he must return to worshiping the one true God. There would be no more rain until God sent it.

Q What did the ravens bring?

A Food for Elijah.

Ahab was angry with God and angry with Elijah for bringing the message. God told Elijah to go to the brook of Cherith where he would be safe and could drink the water from the brook. God sent ravens with bread and meat so that Elijah would not starve.

Q Who shared her food with Elijah?

A The widow in Zarephath.

God told Elijah to go to Zarephath, where a widow would help him. She said she had only enough flour and oil for one more meal, but she agreed to make some bread for Elijah first. When she did, God made sure that there was just enough flour and oil left for the next loaf of bread. For as long as she shared it with Elijah, there was always enough left for more bread. And so God looked after Elijah, the widow, and her son in the drought.

Q Where did Elijah challenge the prophets of Baal?

A On Mount Carmel.

Elijah held a contest. Baal must prove he was god by bringing down fire on the altar. Elijah would ask his God to do the same. Then the people should choose to worship the one true God. Baal failed the challenge. But God brought down fire on Elijah's altar. Then God gave the people rain to end the drought. Elijah's God was the one true God.

THE PROPHETS

Q Why did Naaman wash in the River Jordan?

A Elisha told him it would cure his leprosy.

Naaman was a Syrian army commander. He went to the prophet Elisha because his servant girl told him God could cure him of his terrible skin disease.

Naaman expected a greater miracle than to wash in a dirty river but, when he did so, God cured him.

Q Where did God send Jonah?

A To Nineveh.

Jonah didn't want to go! When he boarded a ship going in the opposite direction, God caused a huge storm at sea. Jonah knew that if the sailors threw him overboard, they would be safe. But God also caused a big fish to swallow Jonah whole, to save him from drowning. Jonah told God he was sorry for running away, and God caused the fish to spit him out. Then Jonah set off for Nineveh with the message God had given him for the people there.

Q Who saw a vision of God in the Temple?

A Isaiah.

Isaiah saw God, surrounded by angelic figures worshiping and singing praises to God. Isaiah was so amazed at how awesome and holy God was that he felt unworthy to be near God. A seraph flew down and touched Isaiah's lips with a burning coal, saying that his sin was forgiven.

God asked for someone to take God's words to the people. Isaiah had only one answer: "Here am I! Send me!"

Q What happened to the dry bones in Ezekiel's vision?

A They became living people.

God told Ezekiel to prophesy to the dry bones. First Ezekiel heard the rattling of the bones as they all joined to each other to make skeletons. Then he watched as tendons and flesh grew on them. God spoke again and breath entered them. Ezekiel saw a huge army of living people—God's people—with renewed life and hope that one day God would bring them out of exile and into their own land once more.

34

DANIEL

Q Where was Daniel exiled?

A In Babylon.

When King Nebuchadnezzar first besieged Jerusalem, he took away some of the treasures from the Temple and a number of young, educated men. They were made to work in the royal palace in Babylon after they had been trained for three years.

Daniel and his three friends, Shadrach, Meshach, and Abednego, were the best of these young men.

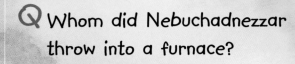

Q Whom did Nebuchadnezzar throw into a furnace?

A Shadrach, Meshach, and Abednego.

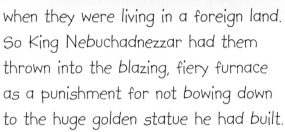

Daniel's three friends refused to bow down and worship anyone but the one true God, even when they were living in a foreign land. So King Nebuchadnezzar had them thrown into the blazing, fiery furnace as a punishment for not bowing down to the huge golden statue he had built.

The men not only survived, but they walked out completely unharmed because God had protected them.

Q What did King Balshazzar see?

A The writing on the wall.

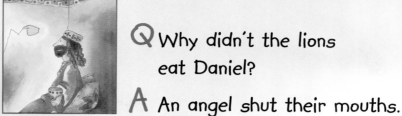

While the King was drinking from the beautiful goblets that his father had stolen from the Temple in Jerusalem, he saw the fingers of a hand write on the plaster of the wall.

Daniel told him that the words meant God had brought Balshazzar's reign to an end because he was not just and good. His Kingdom would be divided among the Medes and Persians. That very night Balshazzar was Killed and his kingdom invaded.

Q Why didn't the lions eat Daniel?

A An angel shut their mouths.

King Darius liked and trusted Daniel but was tricked into having him thrown into the den of lions. His advisers had suggested he make a law that no one should pray to anyone except to him, the King.

Daniel would not pray to anyone except God. He continued to pray three times a day, as was his custom. So when he was thrown to the lions, God Kept him safe, and King

Darius told everyone that Daniel's God had power to save!

NEHEMIAH

Q Which Persian king did Nehemiah serve?

A King Artaxerxes.

Nehemiah had *been exiled to Persia* after the destruction of Jerusalem. He was given the job of cupbearer to the king. He had to taste everything before the king drank it to make sure it was not poisoned.

Q Where did Nehemiah want to go?

A To Jerusalem.

Nehemiah's brother had sent a letter with *bad news.* Although there were *still some of God's people in* Jerusalem, they were being attacked by their enemies because the walls of the city had *been broken down and* the gates destroyed by fire.

Nehemiah was very upset. He wanted to go home and rebuild the city walls.

Q How long did the rebuilding take?

A Fifty-two days!

Nehemiah went to Jerusalem and organized the people into rebuilding the walls and putting up new gates.

The people who lived nearby laughed at what he was trying to do; then they became angry when they saw that the work was taking place. Nehemiah prayed, and he kept working hard. He did not give up.

When the walls were finished, Ezra, the priest, read the law of Moses to the people from a high platform. All the people confessed their sins and worshiped God in Jerusalem once more.

Q What did Nehemiah do?

A He prayed to God.

First, Nehemiah asked God's forgiveness for the sins of his people. Then he asked God for help. If God could make the king let him go, Nehemiah would return to Jerusalem and rebuild it.

A few months later, God answered his prayer. The king noticed that Nehemiah looked sad and asked why. When Nehemiah told him, the king said that he could go to Jerusalem, as long as he came back.

JESUS' BIRTH

Q Who came with a message for Mary?

A The angel Gabriel.

God sent the angel to Nazareth in Galilee with a message for Mary. She was engaged to Joseph, the carpenter, but they were not yet married.

Mary was surprised and afraid, but when she heard that God had chosen her to be the mother of God's Son, she was ready to obey. She promised to accept all that God had planned for her.

Q Where did Mary's baby sleep?

A In a manger.

Mary and Joseph had to travel to Bethlehem. The Roman emperor had ordered a census of all his people. All citizens had to return to the town where they were born and be counted.

When Mary and Joseph reached Bethlehem, the town was so crowded that there was no room for them to stay. But Mary's baby was about to be born. An innkeeper let them use his stable, and that night Mary gave birth to Jesus, her baby son. She laid him in his bed, which was a manger filled with hay for the animals.

Q Why were the
shepherds afraid?

A Angels appeared on the
hillside!

The shepherds were looking after
their sheep when suddenly the night
sky was filled with light. An angel
appeared with good news: the baby
Jesus had been born and was lying
in a manger! More angels appeared,
praising God.

The shepherds ran down the hillside
to Bethlehem. When they found the
baby lying in the manger, they told
everyone they saw
about what the angels
had told them.

Q What did the
wise men bring?

A Gold, frankincense,
and myrrh.

A new star appeared in the skies
when Jesus was born. Wise men in the
east saw it and believed it was a sign
that a new King had been born.

They took gifts and traveled to find
the baby King, following the star until
they came to Bethlehem.

Then they worshiped Jesus and
offered him their gifts.

JESUS' FRIENDS

Q Where was Jesus baptized?

A In the River Jordan.

When Jesus was a grown man, he asked John to baptize him. John baptized people who were sorry for the wrong things they had done.

John baptized Jesus even though he had done nothing wrong.

God was pleased. God said, "This is my Son!"

Q What did the fishermen leave?

A Their fishing nets.

Peter and Andrew had fished all night and caught nothing. Jesus told them to let down their nets in the deeper water of Lake Galilee.

The nets became so full of fish that James and John had to come and help them! Jesus asked all these fishermen to be his disciples, to learn from him, and to help him in his work.

Q Who had Jesus to his house for dinner?

A Matthew.

Matthew was sitting at the tax collector's booth, working for the Romans, when Jesus spoke to him. Matthew got up and followed Jesus, and soon they were eating together in Matthew's house.

The Pharisees disapproved of the people with Jesus. But Jesus told them he had come to help the people who needed him most.

Q Where did Zacchaeus wait?

A Up a tree.

Zacchaeus wanted very much to see Jesus, but he was not tall enough to see over the heads of the crowd. So he climbed up a sycamore tree and watched Jesus walk through the streets of Jericho.

Like Matthew, Zacchaeus collected taxes for the Romans. He had no friends because he cheated people. So when Jesus looked up at him and told Zacchaeus he was coming to his house, everyone was surprised!

Zacchaeus changed when he met Jesus. He promised to give half of what he owned to the poor. He also promised to pay back anyone he had cheated four times the amount.

JESUS' MIRACLES

Q Where did Jesus turn water into wine?

A In Cana, in Galilee.

Mary, Jesus' mother, had been invited to a wedding. Jesus went with his disciples and performed his first miracle there.

When there was no wine left, Jesus turned six large pots of water into the best wine. Everyone was amazed at how good the wine was. Those who knew how it had happened were amazed at what Jesus had done!

Q What made the disciples afraid?

A They thought they were going to drown.

The disciples were sailing across Lake Galilee when a storm began to rage around them. Even the experienced fishermen knew they were in danger.

Jesus was asleep until the frightened men woke him. Jesus told the wind and waves to be still. The storm stopped raging. Jesus had saved the disciples.

Q Who fed over 5000 people?

A Jesus!

Crowds of people had followed Jesus. They wanted to hear his stories; they wanted him to heal them of their illnesses. But they were far from home and Jesus knew they needed to eat.

The disciples brought him five small barley loaves and two little fish. Jesus asked God to bless the food. He gave the food to his disciples, who shared it with the crowd. Everyone had enough to eat, and the disciples collected up twelve baskets of leftovers. It was a miracle!

Q When did Jesus heal a bent-over woman?

A On the sabbath.

Jesus was teaching in the synagogue when he first saw the woman, her back so bent and crooked that she could not look up. When Jesus told her she would be ill no longer, she was able to stand up straight and walk normally.

The leader of the synagogue believed that no healing should be done on the holy sabbath day. But the woman praised God for healing her.

JESUS' TEACHING

Q Where did Jesus start teaching the people?

A In Galilee.

Jesus went to live in Capernaum by Lake Galilee. He healed the people and taught them how God wanted them to live.

Jesus told them to love their enemies and to be generous to people in need. Jesus told them to pray simply and honestly, calling God their father. Jesus told them not to criticize other people, but to ask God to forgive them for the things they had done wrong.

Q What did Jesus teach about God?

A That God loved the people God had made.

Jesus told them not to worry about food and clothing because God loved them even more than God loved the flowers in the fields and the birds in the air. If people tried to please and trust God, God would make sure they had everything they needed.

Q How many friends made a hole in the roof?

A Four.

The men wanted Jesus to heal their friend because he couldn't walk. There were too many people in the house, so they went up the steps to the rooftop and made a large hole. They lowered their friend down in front of Jesus.

"Your sins are forgiven," said Jesus when he saw the man. When people started muttering in disapproval, Jesus went on, "God has the power to heal this man and the power to forgive sins." Then he told the man to pick up his mat and walk.

The man was healed. Jesus had God's power to forgive and to heal.

Q Why did Jesus praise the poor widow?

A She gave all she had to God.

Jesus watched the rich people in the Temple. They were proud and boastful and thought God was pleased with them when they gave lots of money. But Jesus pointed out to his disciples that the widow had given more than the rich people because they gave from their huge wealth and still had lots left over. The woman had given only a few small coins, but she loved God so much she had given all she had.

JESUS' STORIES

Q Where was the kind man from?

A Samaria.

Jesus told a story about a man who was attacked as he walked from Jerusalem to Jericho. Two religious Jews went by without stopping to help him. But a Samaritan, a foreigner, not only stopped and bathed the man's wounds, but also helped him to an inn and paid for his care until he was well enough to travel.

Jesus said this was the way God wanted people to treat each other.

Q Who stored his treasure on earth?

A The rich man.

The story Jesus told was about a rich man who had done so well that he pulled down his barns to build newer and better buildings to store all that he owned. Soon he could relax and enjoy himself because he had everything that he could ever want.

That night the man died. Everything he had stored up for himself was useless. He had spent so much effort thinking about himself that he had not thought about God or cared about other people. Now it was all too late.

Q What did the shepherd lose?

A One of his sheep.

In Jesus' story, the shepherd left 99 of his sheep safely locked up while he went to find the one sheep that had wandered off. All of his sheep were important to him. He cared even if one was lost. Then he called all his friends together to celebrate because he was so happy to find his lost sheep.

Jesus said God loved all God's people as much as the shepherd loved the one sheep.

Q Why did the father throw a party?

A His lost son came home.

The boy wanted to leave home with his share of his inheritance. His father was sad, but he waited patiently.

The boy wasted everything and soon had no friends, money, or food to eat. Feeling sorry for what he had done, he went home. His father was overjoyed to see him and welcomed him back into the family!

Jesus said that God is always waiting for God's children to return and say they're sorry in just the same way.

JESUS' HEALINGS

Q Who needed Jesus to heal his servant?

A A Roman centurion.

The centurion came to Jesus for help, but did not feel he deserved to have Jesus come to his home. He said that a word from Jesus would be enough, even if Jesus could not touch the man who was ill. Jesus healed the centurion's servant because he was amazed at the man's faith.

Q Why did Jairus come to Jesus?

A His little girl was ill.

By the time Jesus came near to Jairus' house, people came to say it was too late. The girl had already died. But Jesus went and took her hand and healed her. She sat up and had something to eat.

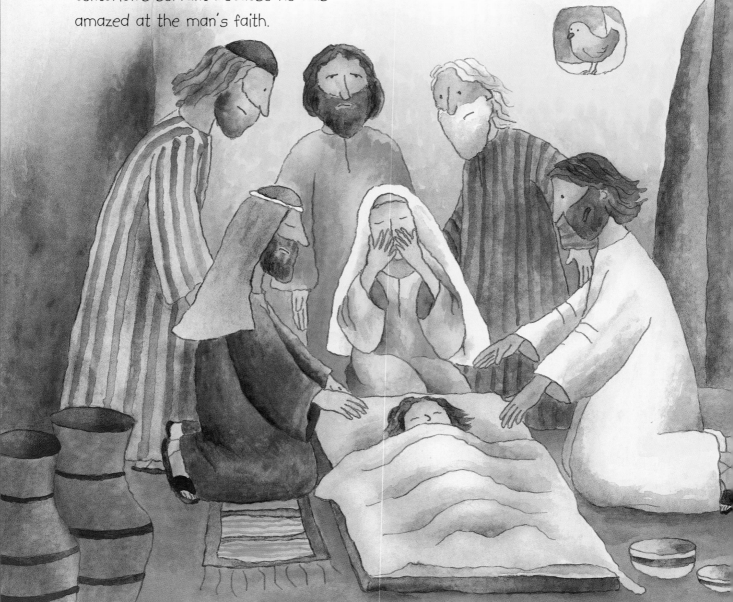

Q How many lepers were healed?

A Ten.

The men stood some distance away from Jesus and shouted to him for help as he entered a village. They had become outcasts because of their skin disease and could not go any closer.

Jesus healed them. He told them to go and show the priests that they were free to go back to their homes and worship God again. Only one of the ten, a Samaritan, came back to thank Jesus and to praise God for healing him.

Q What did Bartimaeus want?

A To see again.

Bartimaeus was begging by the side of the road when Jesus came to Jericho. But he didn't want money from Jesus. Bartimaeus was blind and knew that Jesus had given blind men their sight.

The crowd tried to stop Bartimaeus when he called out to Jesus. They didn't think Jesus would have time for a beggar. But Jesus stopped and listened and asked them to bring the man to him. Jesus healed Bartimaeus and, when the blind man could see, he followed Jesus.

JESUS IN JERUSALEM

Q When did Jesus ride a donkey?

A On his way to Jerusalem.

As Jesus and his disciples approached the city, Jesus asked two of them to go into the village of Bethphage, where they would find a young donkey, and to bring it to him. They went and found the donkey and spread cloaks over its back so Jesus could ride on it to Jerusalem.

Then Jesus rode toward the city gates, where crowds of people welcomed him, cheering and shouting.

Q What did the people wave?

A Palm branches.

They cut branches from the trees and waved them, shouting, "Praise God!" They put their cloaks under the donkey's feet to make a path for Jesus.

Some of the people loved Jesus. They knew Jesus had healed people and given the blind their sight. But the teachers of the Law were angry. They were jealous that so many people listened to Jesus and followed him wherever he went.

Q Who washed Peter's feet?

A Jesus.

Jesus wanted to show his friends how to love one another. A servant usually washed their dusty feet for them. But Jesus took the towel and a bowl of water. He washed his disciples' feet to teach them all how to treat one another kindly.

Jesus said that they should care about one another so much that everyone would know they loved God and lived the way God wanted them to.

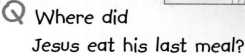

Q Where did Jesus eat his last meal?

A In Jerusalem.

In an upstairs room Jesus broke the bread and asked the disciples to remember his broken body when they ate the Passover meal together. He shared the wine and asked them to remember that his blood would be shed for them.

Judas quietly left the room and went to betray Jesus to his enemies.

JESUS' DEATH

Q Where did the disciples fall asleep?

A In the garden of Gethsemane.

Jesus had taken his friends with him to the Mount of Olives where he had gone to pray each day that week. On Thursday night, he asked them to stay awake and watch with him while he prayed in the garden of Gethsemane. But they kept falling asleep.

Then, led by Judas, the crowd came with clubs and swords to arrest Jesus.

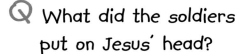

Q What did the soldiers put on Jesus' head?

A A crown of thorns.

Pontius Pilate, the Roman governor, had asked the crowd what he should do with Jesus. They shouted, "Crucify him!" Jesus was handed over to the soldiers.

They made a crown out of thorns and put it on Jesus' head. They made him wear a purple cloak and put a stick in his hand so that he looked like a king or an emperor. Then they mocked him, hit him, and spat on him.

Q Who carried the cross for Jesus?

A Simon of Cyrene.

When the soldiers led Jesus out to be crucified, he carried part of his cross on his back. They forced a man from the crowd to take the cross while they drove Jesus in front of them.

Simon of Cyrene went with Jesus to the place of execution, called Golgotha, or Place of a Skull.

Q How was Jesus killed?

A He was crucified.

The soldiers nailed Jesus to a cross between two thieves. They placed a sign above him saying, "This is Jesus, the King of the Jews." Then the soldiers gambled for his clothes.

Before he died, Jesus spoke to his mother from the cross and to John, his friend and disciple. He asked John to take Mary into his home and look after her; he asked Mary to take John as her son.

JESUS' RESURRECTION

Q Why was the tomb empty?

A Jesus had risen from the dead!

Nicodemus and Joseph of Arimathea had taken the dead body of Jesus down from the cross and buried him in a new tomb in a garden. Then they had rolled a huge stone across the entrance.

Early on Sunday morning, Mary went to the garden with spices to anoint the body. But when she arrived, she found that the stone had been rolled away. Jesus was alive!

Q Where did two disciples walk with Jesus?

A To Emmaus.

Later that day after Mary had seen Jesus alive, two of the disciples walked to the village of Emmaus. A stranger walked along with them. He explained the Scriptures to help the disciples understand that Jesus was the Messiah the prophets had talked about, the one who would save his people.

The disciples asked the man to stay and eat with them when they reached Emmaus. When the man *broke* the bread, they realized that he was Jesus and that he was very much alive!

Q Who touched Jesus' wounds?

A Thomas.

All the other disciples had seen Jesus since he had been raised from the dead, except for Thomas. Thomas knew he could not believe that Jesus was alive unless he saw him for himself.

Jesus came again into a room with a locked door. He wanted Thomas to touch him and know that he was really alive and not a ghost. Thomas was amazed, and he believed.

Q When did Peter jump out of a boat?

A When he saw that the risen Jesus was there!

One night, the disciples went out fishing. They caught nothing; but when morning came, a man on the shore of Lake Galilee told them where to throw the net. They caught 153 fish!

Then they realized that the man was Jesus. He was preparing breakfast on the shore.

Peter jumped into the water, leaving the others to haul in the catch of fish, because he was so pleased to see Jesus again. Peter was sorry that he had pretended he didn't know Jesus. He told Jesus that he loved him and would do anything he asked.

56

PETER

Q When did the Holy Spirit come to the believers?

A On the day of Pentecost.

After Jesus went to be with God in heaven, Peter took care of the believers, about 120 people.

They were in Jerusalem when they heard a great wind blowing and saw tongues of fire resting on each of them. The Holy Spirit gave them power to speak in other languages. They could tell people from all over the world about Jesus' death and resurrection.

Q Where did Peter heal a man who was crippled?

A At the Beautiful Gate.

Peter and John were going to pray in the Temple. As they went in by the Beautiful Gate, a man was being carried there to beg. He had been crippled from birth.

The man asked them for money, but Peter and John had none. Instead, Peter said he would give him a much better gift. Peter healed the man by the power of the Holy Spirit so that he could walk, and jump and run!

Q What did Peter's rooftop vision teach him?

A God's love is for everyone.

Peter had a vision of a sheet covered with all sorts of animals that the Jewish people were forbidden to eat. God told Peter to eat them.

God showed Peter that some of the old laws were now being changed. God needed Peter to understand that God's love was not just for the Jewish people, as everyone had first thought, but reached out to all the people God had made.

Q Who rescued Peter from prison?

A An angel sent by God.

King Herod had arrested Peter and put him in prison, guarded at all times. There were two soldiers standing at the entrance to the prison cell and one on either side of Peter.

Peter's friends were all praying for him because James, one of Jesus' disciples, had already been executed. God answered their prayers. An angel came at night, released Peter from his chains and guided him out of the prison. Doors opened and closed by a miracle. Peter was free!

THE FIRST CHRISTIANS

Q Who was the first
Christian martyr?

A Stephen.

The disciples chose seven men to
help them look after the needs of the
new Christians. Stephen soon became
known among them for the miracles
he was able to perform. He healed
people who were ill and talked about
what Jesus had said and done.

Stephen was arrested and stoned
to death. His last words were a
prayer asking God to forgive the men
who were about to kill him. Paul stood
by and watched Stephen die.

Q How did Philip help
the Ethiopian?

A He explained to
him who Jesus was.

The Ethiopian was the treasurer
of the queen of Ethiopia. He was
traveling to Gaza on his way back
from Jerusalem, where he had gone to
worship God. Philip saw the Ethiopian
sitting in his chariot reading from the
prophet Isaiah.

When Philip explained that Isaiah
was talking about Jesus, the man

wanted to be baptized.
They came to some water
and Philip baptized him
immediately

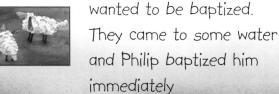

Q Why did Peter go to Joppa?

A To heal Tabitha.

Peter was in nearby Lydda when some of Tabitha's friends came and asked him to help her. She had been well known for her work in helping the poor, but she had become ill and died.

Peter sent all the weeping women away and prayed for Tabitha. Then he turned to Tabitha and asked her to get up. The woman opened her eyes and sat up, completely healed.

Q What job did Cornelius do?

A He was a Roman centurion.

Cornelius had loved and served God for some time, but he did not know Jesus. God told him in a vision to send men to get Peter to come to him.

Peter talked to Cornelius and his friends and family, explaining that Jesus had been sent by God. Jesus had been crucified and then resurrected from the dead so that all who believed in him could have their sins forgiven. The Holy Spirit came to all those in the house who believed and they were baptized, the first Gentiles to become baptized Christians.

PAUL

Q Who met Paul on the road to Damascus?

A Jesus, risen from the dead.

Paul loved God but hated the people who followed Jesus. Paul was on

his way to Damascus to imprison more of the believers when he saw flashing lights and fell to the ground. He could not see, but he heard the voice of Jesus asking, "Why are you persecuting me, Paul?"

His friends took Paul to Damascus where Ananias came and restored his sight. Then Paul was baptized a Christian.

Q Where was Paul when he baptized Lydia?

A In Philippi.

God had chosen Paul to tell the Gentiles why Jesus had to die so that sins could be forgiven.

Paul had traveled to Philippi in Macedonia where there was no synagogue. When he and his friends went to the river to pray on the sabbath, they met Lydia, a trader in purple cloth, and some other women. After Paul had talked to them, they

became believers and were baptized.

Q Why did the jailer want to kill himself?

A He thought his prisoners had escaped.

Paul and Silas had been beaten and thrown into prison.

They didn't get angry; they prayed and sang hymns to God while the other prisoners listened. Then, at midnight, God sent an earthquake that loosened their chains and opened the prison doors.

The Philippian jailer was woken by the noise of the earthquake. Paul stopped him from harming himself and told him how he could be saved by believing in Jesus.

Q What happened to Paul on his way to Rome?

A He was shipwrecked!

Paul made many enemies because he spoke the truth about Jesus. When Paul was taken prisoner by the Romans, they had to send him to Rome to stand trial.

The journey by sea was difficult. When the ship was hit by a storm, the sailors thought they would all die. The boat was shipwrecked off the island of Malta, but everyone survived.

Paul reached Rome. He shared what he knew about Jesus with all those who would listen. Many Romans became believers and started to follow Jesus.

Index of Bible Stories: